THE MYSTERY
OF MANOR HALL

Tom and Milly are staying at Manor Hall with Uncle Henry. Uncle Henry doesn't like teenagers, and he sometimes looks angry. Manor Hall is an old dark house with a mystery. There is a beautiful music room. But the music room is always locked and has 'Do Not Enter' on the door.

One evening there is a full moon. At midnight Tom and Milly hear something. They can hear someone singing, and the noise is coming from the music room.

Who is singing in the music room?

What is the mystery of Manor Hall?

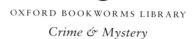

OXFORD BOOKWORMS LIBRARY

Crime & Mystery

The Mystery of Manor Hall

Starter (250 headwords)

JANE CAMMACK

The Mystery
of Manor Hall

Illustrated by
Jérôme Mireault

OXFORD UNIVERSITY PRESS

OXFORD
UNIVERSITY PRESS

Great Clarendon Street, Oxford, OX2 6DP, United Kingdom

Oxford University Press is a department of the University of Oxford.
It furthers the University's objective of excellence in research, scholarship,
and education by publishing worldwide. Oxford is a registered trade
mark of Oxford University Press in the UK and in certain other countries

ISBN: 978 0 19 478599 0   Book
ISBN: 978 0 19 462031 4   Book and audio pack

Printed in China

Word count (main text): 1,390 words

For more information on the Oxford Bookworms Library,
visit www.oup.com/elt/gradedreaders

ACKNOWLEDGEMENTS

Illustrated by Jérôme Mireault, colagene.com
Cover image by mRGB courtesy of Shutterstock

CONTENTS

The Mystery of Manor Hall

'We don't want to stay with Uncle Henry, Mum.' The boy with dark hair and blue eyes takes his mobile phone out of his pocket. 'Grandma says he doesn't like teenagers.'

His mother shakes her head and Tom looks out the window again. The car goes left. The sign on the gate says 'Manor Hall'.

'Manor Hall,' says the beautiful girl sitting next to her brother Tom. 'Does Uncle Henry live here?'

Her mother hears what Milly says. 'Henry is strange, but he's nice, too.'

'Can't we come to the new house with you, Mum? We can help,' Milly asks.

'No, Milly,' says her mum. 'There aren't any beds in the new house.'

The car stops. 'Here we are,' says Mum.

The house is very old and dark. There are lots of small windows. Milly is afraid.

A man opens the door. He is old and he has got white hair and big eyebrows. He looks at Tom and Milly with his grey eyes.

'You're late,' he says. 'Come in.'

'Sorry,' says Tom. 'I'm Tom. How do you do?'

The old man looks angry.

'And I'm Milly,' says Milly. 'Your house is very big.'

'It is,' says Uncle Henry. 'You can explore, but there is one room where you can't go.'

3

They walk along a corridor and see a sitting room where there are beautiful sofas, and pictures on the walls.

Then they come to a door.

'This is the music room,' says Uncle Henry. There is a sign on the door. It says 'Do Not Enter'.

'Why can't we go in there?' asks Milly. 'I can play the piano, and I love music.'

Uncle Henry shakes his head. 'I can't tell you. But never open this door!'

'What a strange man,' Tom says when they are in their bedroom. 'Why can't we go into the music room?'

But Milly isn't listening. 'Let's explore!' she says.

Tom and Milly walk up and down and open doors. Then they come to the music room. Tom is about to open the door when Uncle Henry sees them.

'Get away from there!' shouts Uncle Henry.

Later, when they are having dinner in the dining room, Uncle Henry is very quiet.

'Are you angry with us?' asks Milly.

Uncle Henry doesn't answer. He shakes his head. Then he says, 'There's a full moon tonight.'

He gets up and looks out the window. 'Lock your bedroom door,' he says, 'and don't open it.'

'I don't understand,' Milly says to Tom. 'Why does Uncle Henry look at the moon? Why can't we go into the music room? It's a mystery.'

Tom isn't listening. He's reading a book.

'I want to explore,' Tom says suddenly.

'We can't!' says Milly.

It's midnight and Milly wakes up. It's very dark in the bedroom and she can hear a noise. She gets out of bed and goes to her brother's bed.

'Tom, Tom,' she says and shakes his arm. Tom opens his eyes. 'Milly, it's late. Go back to bed.' He closes his eyes again.

'No, Tom, get up! There's a strange noise.'

Tom goes to the door and listens. 'You're right,' he says to Milly. 'I can hear someone singing.'

'Can Uncle Henry sing?' Milly asks Tom. Tom laughs, 'Let's see.' He opens the door.

'No!' Milly says. 'There's a full moon. We can't go out.'

'You can stay here, but I want to see who's singing at midnight.' Tom opens the door and they run into the corridor.

'Someone is singing in the music room,' says Milly.

'You're right,' says Tom. 'It's a man and he's singing a song about the sea.'

'It's beautiful,' says Milly. 'Is it Uncle Henry?'

Tom isn't listening. He opens the door of the music room and goes in.

'Don't, Tom!' says Milly. 'We can't go into the music room!'

The music room is very big and Milly is afraid.

'We haven't got much time before Uncle Henry hears us,' she says.

Tom puts the light on and the singing stops.

In the music room there's a piano and there are lots of pictures on the wall. But Uncle Henry isn't there. Milly wants to go.

On one wall there is a very big picture of a ship. Milly and Tom look at the picture and they can see that the sea is moving. They can hear the water.

There is a man standing on the ship. He has got long black hair and a black hat. He is singing a song about the sea. He's a pirate.

Tom and Milly are afraid, but they can't move. The pirate looks at them. He stops singing and he smiles. Suddenly he comes out of the picture and into the music room.

'Help!' shouts Milly.

Milly looks at the handsome pirate. He has a big hat, and is very white.

'He's a ghost,' she says in a quiet voice to Tom. 'Tom, let's go.'

Tom doesn't answer. The pirate is near the door so they can't go.

'Who's in my music room?' the pirate shouts. 'This is my room!'

'You're right,' says Tom. 'This is your music room and we're going to bed.'

The pirate shakes his head. 'Oh no you're not! Sit down. I'm going to tell you my story.'

'My name is William Bones, but everyone calls me Billy,' says the pirate.

'The year is 1793. My men and I sail the seven seas in my ship *The Pearl*. We fight pirate ships and we sing songs about the sea. We are very happy because we have lots of treasure.'

'Then one day I help an old woman and she paints a picture of my ship. "This picture's magic," she tells me. "Before you die, put it in a house near the sea. When you die and the moon is full, your ghost can sail your ship for one night." Then the old woman looks at me and she says, "Pirate Billy Bones, remember that the picture must be near the sea."'

'Now it's 1850,' Billy says. 'When I'm old, I die in my house by the sea. The old woman is right. When the moon is full, my ghost can sail my ship for one night.'

1910

'But then in 1910 someone brings the picture here to Manor Hall,' the pirate says. 'This house isn't near the sea, so I can't sail my ship. When the moon is full, I sing songs about the sea, and the people in the house are afraid. They are afraid of the ghost. They put my picture in the music room and lock the door.'

Suddenly the door of the music room opens.

Uncle Henry stands there. He looks at Billy Bones and then at Tom and Milly. His face is white.

'Oh dear,' he says. 'Now you know about the mystery!'

'Now I must tell you my story,' says Uncle Henry.

'The year is 1976. I buy this house from an old man. He tells me about the picture and the ghost in the music room. I'm afraid of ghosts and I don't go into the music room. I lock the door.'

'Every month when there is a full moon, I hear a pirate singing songs about the sea,' says Uncle Henry.

'I know that he is unhappy and I know that he wants to go back to the sea. But I'm afraid and I can't help him.'

'I know!' says Tom. 'Our new house is in a beautiful place near the sea,' he says. 'From my bedroom I can hear the seagulls and the waves. Come with us. We can put your picture in the breakfast room where you can see the sea.'

Uncle Henry begins to smile.

'How wonderful,' says Billy Bones.

'I'm happy that you want to go with Tom and Milly,' says Uncle Henry. 'Please sit down, Billy Bones, and listen.'

Everyone sits at the kitchen table. 'You can go, but you must be quiet. You must sing quietly in their new house.'

'All right,' says Billy Bones. 'Are you afraid of ghosts now, Henry?'

Henry smiles. 'No, I'm not, Billy.'

'Mum's here,' says Milly. They run out of the house.

'Mum, we have something from Uncle Henry,' says Milly. 'It's for the new house.'

Mum looks at the picture. 'A ship and a handsome pirate . . . how lovely,' says Mum.

Tom and Milly say goodbye to Uncle Henry.

They take the picture to their new house by the sea. Pirate Billy Bones stands on his ship and he looks at his new home. He can hear seagulls and he quietly sings a song about the sea.

One day when there is a full moon . . . his ship disappears.

GLOSSARY

dinner the main meal of the day (usually in the evening)

disappear to go away suddenly

explore to travel around a place to learn about it

eyebrows the hair above your eyes

fight *(v)* to attack someone

full moon the moon when it looks like a circle

ghost a dead person that moves around and people can see or hear it

handsome *(adj)* a man who is nice to look at

lock *(v)* to close something with a key *(adj)* **locked**

magic a special power that can make impossible things happen

music room a place where you play the piano, sing, etc.

mystery something we do not understand

pirate a person who fights ships on the sea to get treasure

sail *(v)* to travel on water in a boat or ship

seagull a bird that lives near the sea

shake to move your head from side to side to say 'no'

ship a large boat

song words that you sing

treasure a collection of gold, silver, jewellery, etc.

unhappy sad

waves lines of water that move across the sea

The Mystery of Manor Hall

ACTIVITIES

Before Reading

1 Look at the front cover of the book and answer these questions.

1 Where do you think the story happens?
   a ☐ in a modern house
   b ☐ in an old house
   c ☐ in an apartment

2 Where do you think Manor Hall is?
   a ☐ America
   b ☐ South Korea
   c ☐ England

2 Read the back cover of the book and answer the questions.

1 Which room can nobody go in?
2 What do Tom and Milly hear?
3 What is moving in a picture?
4 Who is in the music room?

While Reading

1 Read pages 1–5 then answer these questions.

1 Where does Uncle Henry live?
2 Who is going to stay with Uncle Henry?
3 What does their grandma say about Uncle Henry?
4 Where is their mum going?
5 Does Milly like the house? Why/Why not?
6 Are Tom and Milly early?

2 Read pages 6–10. Are these sentences true (T) or false (F)?

1 At dinner Uncle Henry talks a lot.   T   F
2 Milly is reading a book in bed.   T   F
3 Milly wakes up at midnight.   T   F
4 There's a full moon.   T   F
5 They can hear a woman singing a song
  about the sea.   T   F

3 Read pages 11–14 and answer these questions.

Who . . .   1 . . . puts the light on?
               2 . . . is singing a song about the sea?
               3 . . . shouts 'help'?
               4 . . . is very white?
               5 . . . listens to a story?

4 Read pages 15–18, then match the sentence halves to make four complete sentences.

1 In 1793 Billy Bones and his men . . .
2 An old woman . . .
3 In 1910 . . .
4 The people at Manor Hall . . .

a someone takes the picture to Manor Hall.
b paints a magic picture.
c are afraid of ghosts.
d fight pirates.

5 Read pages 19–21 and answer the questions.

1 Who comes into the music room?
2 When does Uncle Henry buy Manor Hall?
3 What is Uncle Henry afraid of?
4 Who says 'I can't help him.'
5 What can Tom hear from his bedroom?

6 Guess what happens next in the story.   *Yes*   *No*

1 Billy Bones doesn't want Tom and Milly
  to take the picture.   ☐   ☐
2 Tom and Milly's mother doesn't want
  the picture.   ☐   ☐
3 Uncle Henry wants Billy Bones to stay.   ☐   ☐
4 Tom and Milly take the picture to their
  house by the sea.   ☐   ☐

31

After Reading

1 **What do you know about Billy Bones and Uncle Henry? Choose the right words for each person, and then write a description.**

> *long black hair / a black hat*
> *white hair / big eyebrows*
> *handsome / pirate*
> *full moon / sails ship*
> *afraid / ghosts*
> *buys Manor Hall / 1976*

2 **The Story of Pirate Billy Bones. Put the sentences in the correct order. Number them 1–10.**

a ☐ When the moon is full the ghost can sail for one night.

b ☐ Billy sings songs and the people at Manor Hall are afraid.

c ☐ They fight other pirates.

d ☐ Billy dies in 1850.

e ☐ In 1793 Billy and his men sail their ship *The Pearl*.

f ☐ In 1910 someone takes the picture to Manor Hall.

g ☐ An old woman paints a picture of *The Pearl*.

h ☐ The house isn't near the sea.

i ☐ The picture must be near the sea.

j ☐ The picture is magic.

3 Use these words to join the sentences together.

but   when   because   and   for

1 'You can explore. There is one room where you can't go.'
2 Tom is about to open the door. Uncle Henry sees them.
3 Tom opens the door. They run into the corridor.
4 We are very happy. We have lots of treasure.
5 When the moon is full my ghost can sail my ship. One night.

4 Complete this summary of the story. Use these words.

when   take   moon   because   comes
room   in   unhappy   tells   near

Tom and Milly are at Manor Hall, but there is a mystery. Uncle Henry says that they can explore, but there is one _____ where they can't go. One night, when the _____ is full, they hear someone singing in the music room. They go _____ . There is a picture of a ship and a pirate and the ship is moving. The pirate _____ out of the picture. He _____ Tom and Milly his story. He is _____ because Manor Hall isn't _____ the sea. He can't sail his ship _____ the moon is full. Tom and Milly _____ the picture home with them. The pirate is happy _____ their house is near the sea.

ABOUT THE AUTHOR

Jane Cammack was born in London, but now lives in Henley-on-Thames. She was an opera singer before becoming a writer and performed at *Sadler's Wells* and *Glyndebourne*. She lived in Italy for some years and sang at *La Scala* in Milan.

She has written several original stories for readers and enjoys writing fantasy. She has adapted and retold popular classics and has written many culture books and summer holiday books. In her free time she likes walking in the woods with her dog, reading, and travelling.

OXFORD BOOKWORMS LIBRARY

Classics • Crime & Mystery • Factfiles • Fantasy & Horror
Human Interest • Playscripts • Thriller & Adventure
True Stories • World Stories

The OXFORD BOOKWORMS LIBRARY provides enjoyable reading in English, with a wide range of classic and modern fiction, non-fiction, and plays. It includes original and adapted texts in seven carefully graded language stages, which take learners from beginner to advanced level. An overview is given on the next pages.

All Stage 1 titles are available as audio recordings, as well as over eighty other titles from Starter to Stage 6. All Starters and many titles at Stages 1 to 4 are specially recommended for younger learners. Every Bookworm is illustrated, and Starters and Factfiles have full-colour illustrations.

The OXFORD BOOKWORMS LIBRARY also offers extensive support. Each book contains an introduction to the story, notes about the author, a glossary, and activities. Additional resources include tests and worksheets, and answers for these and for the activities in the books. There is advice on running a class library, using audio recordings, and the many ways of using Oxford Bookworms in reading programmes. Resource materials are available on the website <www.oup.com/bookworms>.

The *Oxford Bookworms Collection* is a series for advanced learners. It consists of volumes of short stories by well-known authors, both classic and modern. Texts are not abridged or adapted in any way, but carefully selected to be accessible to the advanced student.

You can find details and a full list of titles in the *Oxford Bookworms Library Catalogue* and *Oxford English Language Teaching Catalogues*, and on the website <www.oup.com/bookworms>.

STARTER • 250 HEADWORDS

present simple – present continuous – imperative –
can/cannot, must – going to (future) – simple gerunds …

Her phone is ringing – but where is it?

Sally gets out of bed and looks in her bag. No phone. She looks under the bed. No phone. Then she looks behind the door. There is her phone. Sally picks up her phone and answers it. *Sally's Phone*

STAGE 1 • 400 HEADWORDS

… past simple – coordination with *and*, *but*, *or* – subordination with *before*, *after*, *when*, *because*, *so* …

I knew him in Persia. He was a famous builder and I worked with him there. For a time I was his friend, but not for long. When he came to Paris, I came after him – I wanted to watch him. He was a very clever, very dangerous man. *The Phantom of the Opera*

STAGE 2 • 700 HEADWORDS

… present perfect – *will* (future) – *(don't) have to, must not, could* – comparison of adjectives – simple *if* clauses – past continuous – tag questions – *ask/tell* + infinitive …

While I was writing these words in my diary, I decided what to do. I must try to escape. I shall try to get down the wall outside. The window is high above the ground, but I have to try. I shall take some of the gold with me – if I escape, perhaps it will be helpful later. *Dracula*

... should, may – present perfect continuous – *used to* – past perfect –
causative – relative clauses – indirect statements ...

Of course, it was most important that no one should see
Colin, Mary, or Dickon entering the secret garden. So Colin
gave orders to the gardeners that they must all keep away
from that part of the garden in future. ***The Secret Garden***

STAGE 4 • 1400 HEADWORDS

... past perfect continuous – passive (simple forms) –
would conditional clauses – indirect questions –
relatives with *where/when* – gerunds after prepositions/phrases ...

I was glad. Now Hyde could not show his face to the world
again. If he did, every honest man in London would be
proud to report him to the police. ***Dr Jekyll and Mr Hyde***

STAGE 5 • 1800 HEADWORDS

... future continuous – future perfect –
passive (modals, continuous forms) –
would have conditional clauses – modals + perfect infinitive ...

If he had spoken Estella's name, I would have hit him. I was so
angry with him, and so depressed about my future, that I could
not eat the breakfast. Instead I went straight to the old house.
Great Expectations

STAGE 6 • 2500 HEADWORDS

... passive (infinitives, gerunds) – advanced modal meanings –
clauses of concession, condition

When I stepped up to the piano, I was confident. It was as if
I knew that the prodigy side of me really did exist. And when I
started to play, I was so caught up in how lovely I looked that I
didn't worry how I would sound. ***The Joy Luck Club***

The Girl with Green Eyes

JOHN ESCOTT

Greg is a porter at the Shepton Hotel in New York.

When a girl with beautiful green eyes asks him for help, Greg can't say no.

The girl's name is Cassie, and she says she is an artist. She tells Greg that her stepfather has her sketchbooks, and now she wants them back.

Cassie also says her stepfather is staying at Greg's hotel . . . so what could go wrong?

Dead Man's Money

JOHN ESCOTT

When Cal Dexter rents one of the Blue Lake Cabins, he finds $3000 – under the floor! He doesn't know it, but it is the money from a bank robbery. A dead man's money.

'Do I take it to the police?' he thinks.

But three more people want the money, and two of them are dangerous.

Pirate Treasure

PHILLIP BURROWS AND MARK FOSTER

Tom Creek's treasure is under the sea. Many men try to get the treasure, but many men die.

'Our boat is ready. We are all good divers. Let's find the treasure! Yes?' says John West to his wife and friends. 'Yes! Arr! Ooohh!' they shout.

They are all ready to go – but are they afraid of Tom Creek's curse?

The Girl with Red Hair

CHRISTINE LINDOP

Every day people come to Mason's store – old people, young people, men and women.

From his office, and in the store, Mark watches them. And when they leave the store, he forgets them.

Then one day a girl with red hair comes to the store, and everything changes for Mark. Now he can't forget that beautiful face, those green eyes, and that red hair . . .

Les Misérables
Retold by Jennifer Bassett

France, 1815. Jean Valjean leaves prison after nineteen years. These are dangerous and troubled times, and life is hard. Valjean must begin a new life, but how can he escape his past, and his enemy, Inspector Javert?

This story for Bookworms is loosely based on the famous novel *Les Misérables* by Victor Hugo, one of France's greatest writers. The novel was written in 1862, and the story has been retold many times – in a musical, in plays for radio and theatre, and in more than fifty films for television and cinema.

Shirley Homes and the Lithuanian Case
JENNIFER BASSETT

Shirley Homes is a private investigator. She is clever with computers, and knows London like the back of her hand. She laughs when people say, 'Was Sherlock Holmes your grandfather?' Sherlock Holmes, of course, was not a real person, but, like Sherlock, Shirley has good eyes, and good ears. And she knows the right questions to ask.

And in the Lithuanian Case, the right questions are important. Because Shirley must find a missing person – Carrie Williams, aged fifteen. Where is she? Who is she with?